Welcome

To Julian & Sophia,

Stay Awesome!

Lee Bolling

10/27/20

to Earth
Fellow Human

by Lee Bolling

Thank you to all my family and friends
for making this book a reality.

Welcome to Earth Fellow Human
Written and Illustrated by Lee Bolling

Published by Lee Bolling

www.welcometoearth.net

ISBN 978-1-7351107-0-7

For Max, Thomas, Clare,
and my fellow humans

years ago = ya
million years ago = mya = 1,000,000 ya
billion years ago = bya = 1,000,000,000 ya

Welcome to Earth, fellow human!

This is our home planet. Our home base.

At this very moment, we are zipping through space faster than a speeding bullet.

Our Earth is the only place that has life, as far as we know.

The rest of outer space is too cold or too hot. Or doesn't have air or water for us to survive.

That's why we must keep our home base in good working order.

We can't live without our planet.

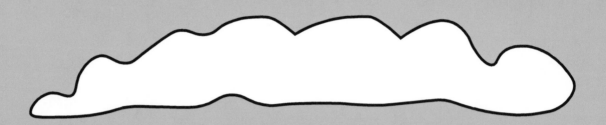

So where did the Earth come from? And how did we
end up here?

In order to tell this fantastic story, we need to go back
13.8 billion years ago to the very beginning of the
universe.

Imagine that your body is the timeline of the universe.

The universe starts at the bottom of your feet. ─────────────

And the present moment, right now, is at the top of your head. Your body timeline will help you remember this amazing story.

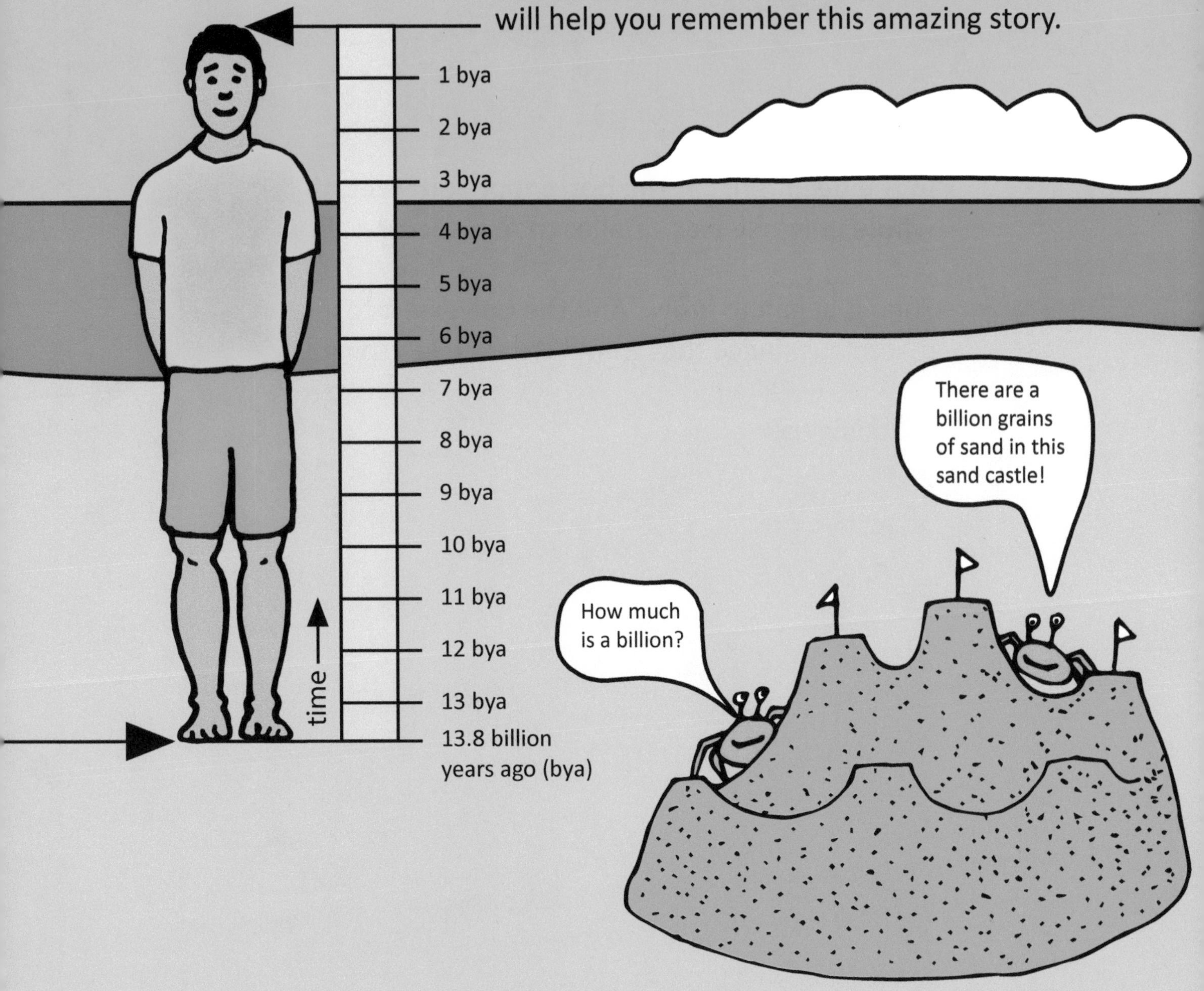

In the beginning, at the bottom of your feet, the whole universe was smaller than a soccer ball.

Then it began to grow. And the universe began a marvelous dance that would create everything...

Including us.

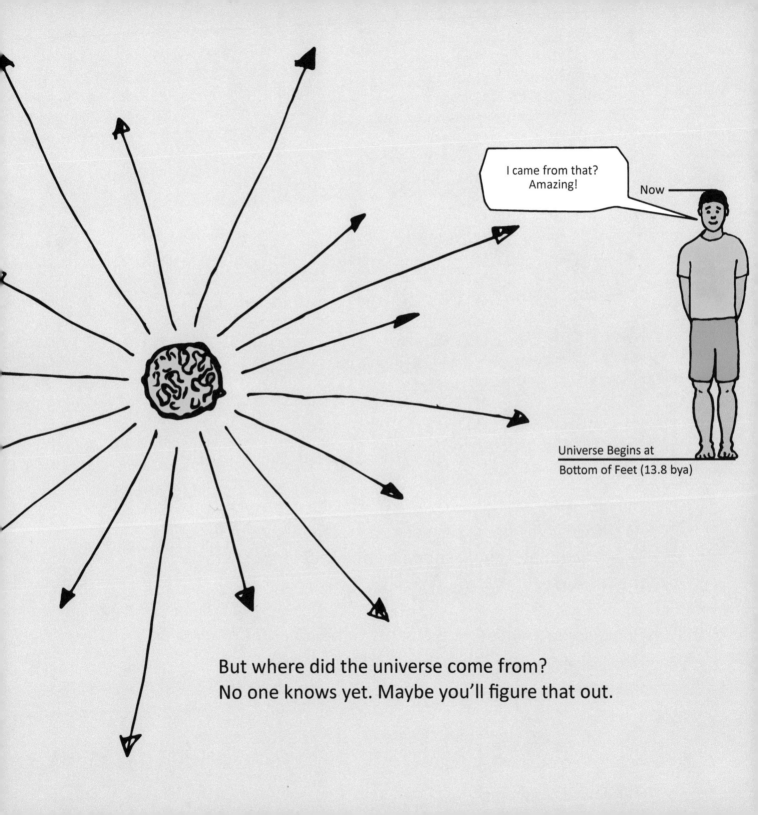

But where did the universe come from?
No one knows yet. Maybe you'll figure that out.

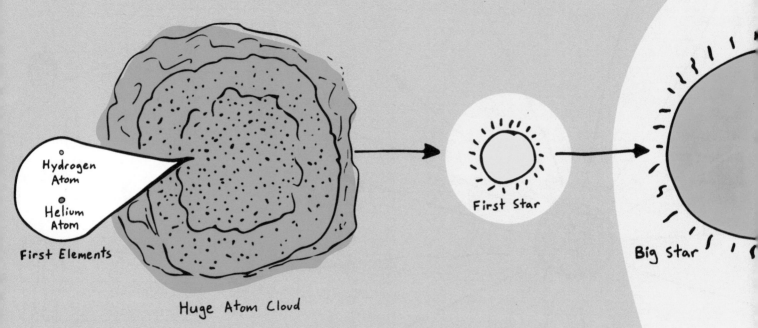

Hydrogen
Atom

Helium
Atom

First Elements

Huge Atom Cloud

First Star

Big Star

As the universe grew, the very first elements were formed. These elements would soon become the building blocks of the universe.

Huge clouds of the first elements came together to form the first stars, and the first light spread across the dark universe.

The stars grew bigger and bigger as they aged until they finally exploded.

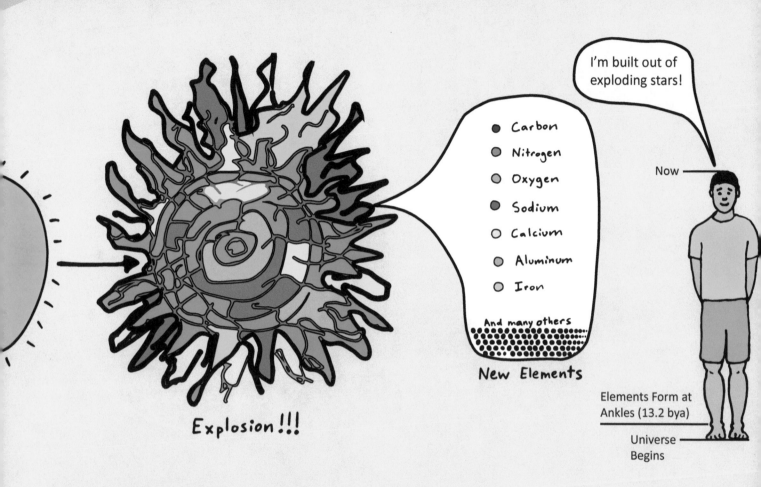

These exploding stars were so powerful that the first elements smashed and fused together to make brand new types of elements.

Everything is built out of these elements. Your body, your food, your house, the Earth, everything.

Exploding stars created all these different elements by the time we reach your ankles.

That is why we can say we're made from the stars.

Our Galaxy

Universe

Over time, billions and billions of new stars formed out of the elements.

The stars clustered together to form galaxies. Soon there would be billions of galaxies across the universe. That's a lot of stars!

Our very own galaxy was formed at your knees and holds billions of stars and planets inside of it.

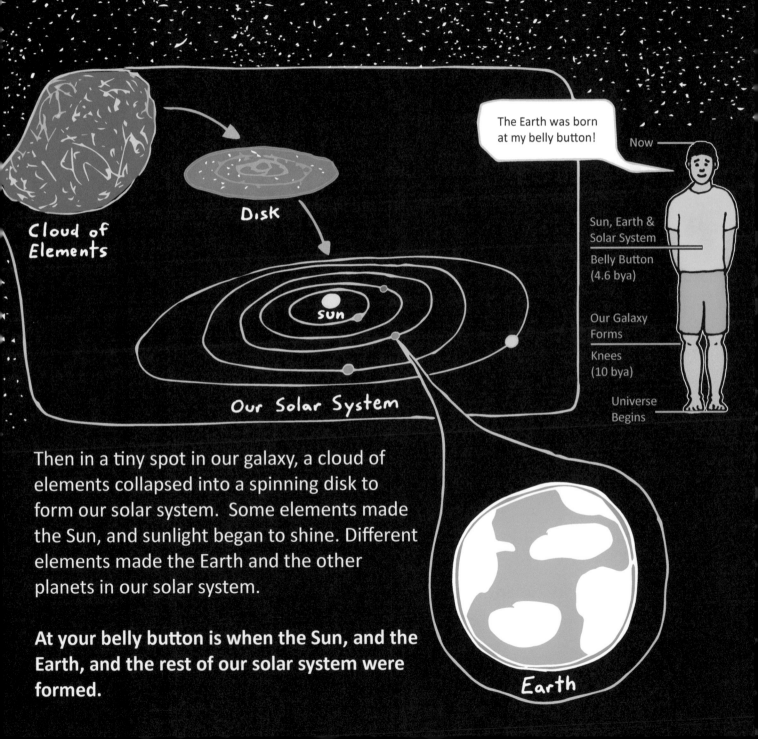

Cloud of Elements

Disk

Our Solar System

Sun

The Earth was born at my belly button!

Now

Sun, Earth & Solar System
Belly Button (4.6 bya)

Our Galaxy Forms
Knees (10 bya)

Universe Begins

Earth

Then in a tiny spot in our galaxy, a cloud of elements collapsed into a spinning disk to form our solar system. Some elements made the Sun, and sunlight began to shine. Different elements made the Earth and the other planets in our solar system.

At your belly button is when the Sun, and the Earth, and the rest of our solar system were formed.

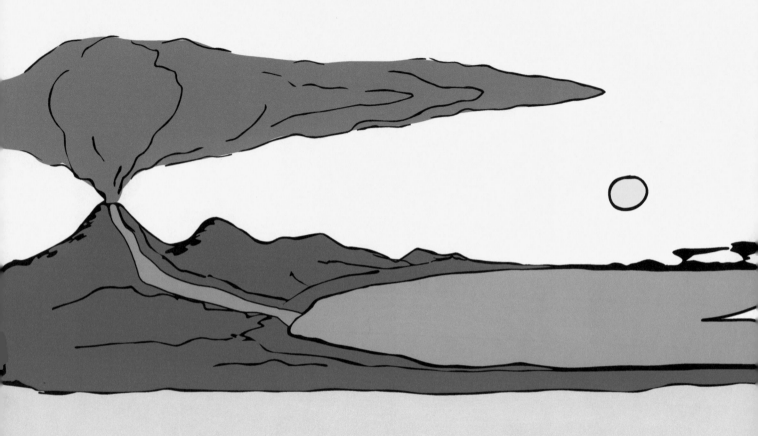

But our brand-new Earth looked nothing like it does today.

It was covered in rock. There was no oxygen to breathe or food to eat.

Nothing was alive.

Luckily, our planet was covered with huge oceans of water, which was a key ingredient for building life.

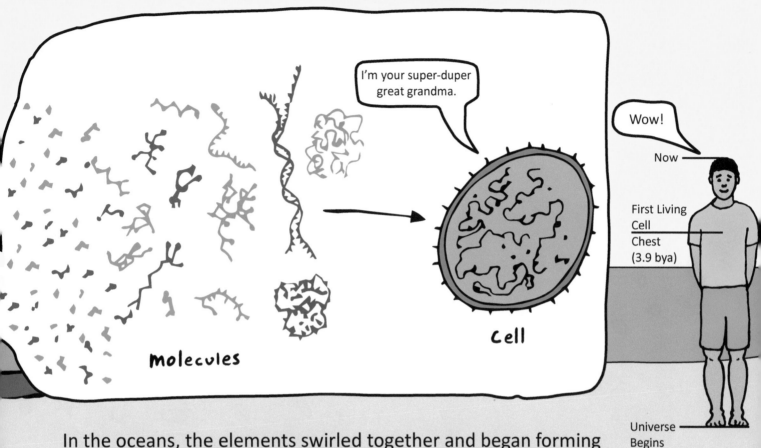

In the oceans, the elements swirled together and began forming little molecules. Molecules are like tiny machines with all sorts of amazing shapes and movements.

Over time, these molecules formed the very first living thing, called the cell.

This was the first life on Earth! The first living cell was formed by the time we reach your chest.

This cell would reproduce and evolve over time to create all of the living things on our planet, including us.

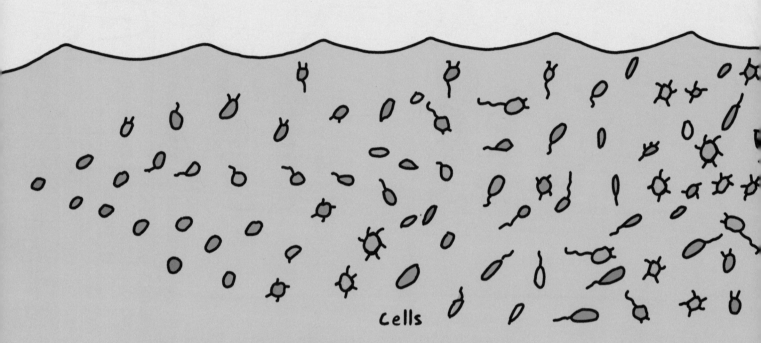

Cells

Soon the oceans were filled with billions of tiny living cells.

Some cells evolved tails for swimming. Other cells just floated along eating whatever molecules came their way.

But the most amazing cells were the ones able to grow from the Sun's light, using photosynthesis. They used the Sun's energy to grow and, at the same time, released oxygen into the air.

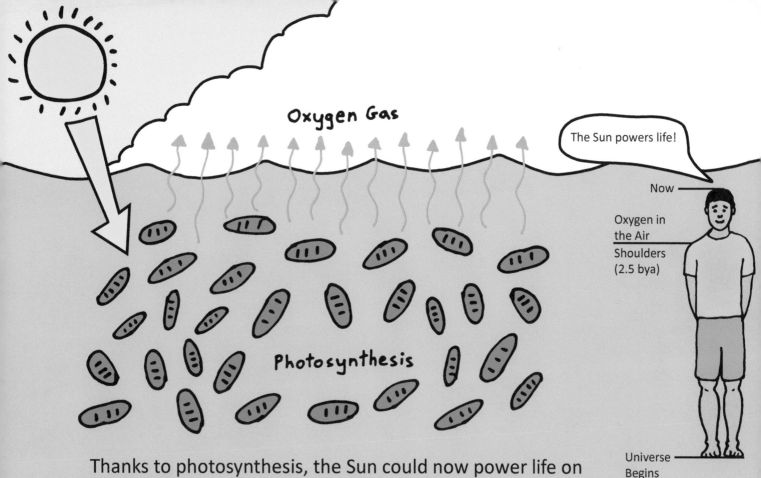

Thanks to photosynthesis, the Sun could now power life on Earth. More Sun-powered cells grew, and they created more food for other hungry cells.

And more oxygen was pumped into the air, which future lifeforms, like us, could breathe.

Pretty soon, the Earth's air was filled with oxygen, which happened at your shoulders.

Take a deep breath.
You're breathing in oxygen, powered by the Sun.

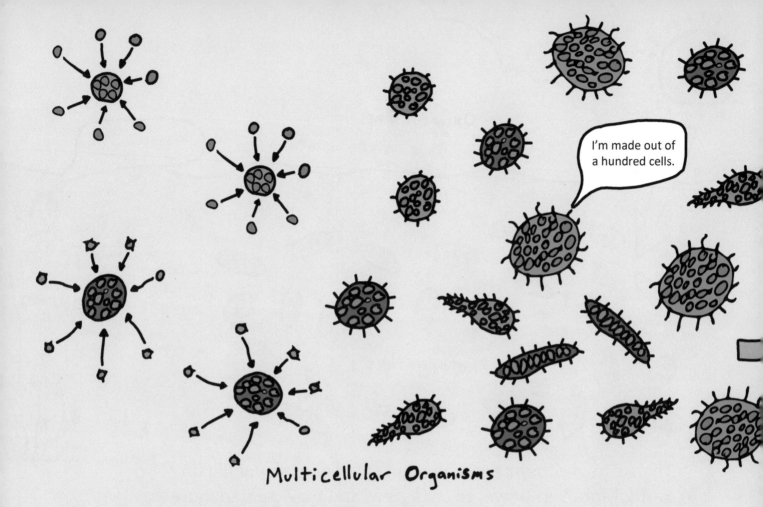

Multicellular Organisms

Cells are super small. So small that you can't see them with your bare eyes.

So how did life get bigger?

Over time, a group of cells evolved into a new lifeform that was made out of many cells, not just one.

These are called multicellular organisms, which formed by the time we reach your mouth.

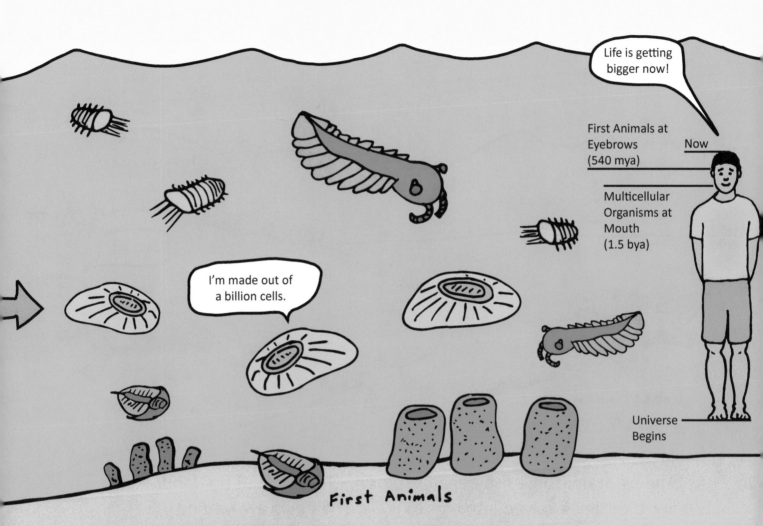

From this point on, bigger and bigger life forms could evolve.
Now, an organism could be made up of billions of cells.

This led to the very first ocean animals, which evolved by the time we reach your eyebrows.

Soon, the oceans were teaming with all sorts of amazing life, like fish and other wild creatures.

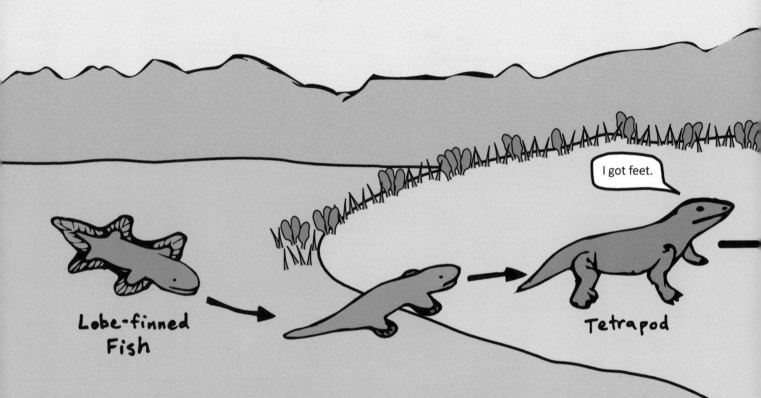

Lobe-finned Fish

Tetrapod

I got feet.

As time went on, some fish began exploring the edges of the land. Slowly, their fins evolved into legs to walk. Their gills evolved into lungs to breathe oxygen in the air. Now they could climb out of the ocean and live on the land for the first time.

Plants moved onto the land, too, and pumped even more oxygen into the air.

The first land animals and land plants began when we reach your forehead.

The animals began to roam the land and evolved into all types of marvelous creatures. Some of them became the dinosaurs and birds. Others evolved into the first mammals.

The dinosaurs lived just a thumb's width from the top of your head.

Unfortunately for the dinosaurs, a giant asteroid smashed our planet, killing much of the life on Earth and causing all the dinosaurs to go extinct.

Luckily our ancestors, the mammals, were able to survive and thrive.

First Mammal

Primate

With the dinosaurs gone, the first mammals spread across the land as life grew back. Over time, they evolved into many different types of creatures, like elephants, whales, carnivores, rodents and rabbits.

Some of the mammals evolved into our ancestors, called primates, which walked on all four feet.

Soon, our ancestors evolved to walk upright on just two feet. This allowed them to travel further and use their hands for making tools out of wood and stones, and for hunting and gathering food.

Then our ancestors discovered how to make fire. This happened in the thickness of a single one of your hairs.

Fire was their most important discovery. Food could be cooked, and better tools could be built. Even today, no other animal has learned how to make fire.

Fire
600,000 ya

Homo
Erectus

Bigger Brains

First

300,000 ya

With their fire and tools, our ancestors became much more powerful. And they too evolved in the land around them. Thanks to cooking, they could eat better food and didn't need to chew as much. Soon their jaws shrank, and their brains grew bigger and more complex, giving each generation more powerful thinking.

With their newly aquired smarts, they evolved into the very first humans. **This is how we humans evolved on earth! We didn't show up until half the thickness of a single human hair.**

We developed language to tell stories to each other and imagine new ideas, which allowed us to live together in larger groups.

We learned how to grow more food in farms, to have more food to eat. Slowly, we explored and populated the whole Earth. We created all sorts of awesome ideas and amazing inventions.

That brings us to today, right now, which is at the top of your head.

This is how the Earth was formed and how we humans came to be.

From the bottom of your feet to the top of your head, now you can remember the story of where we came from.

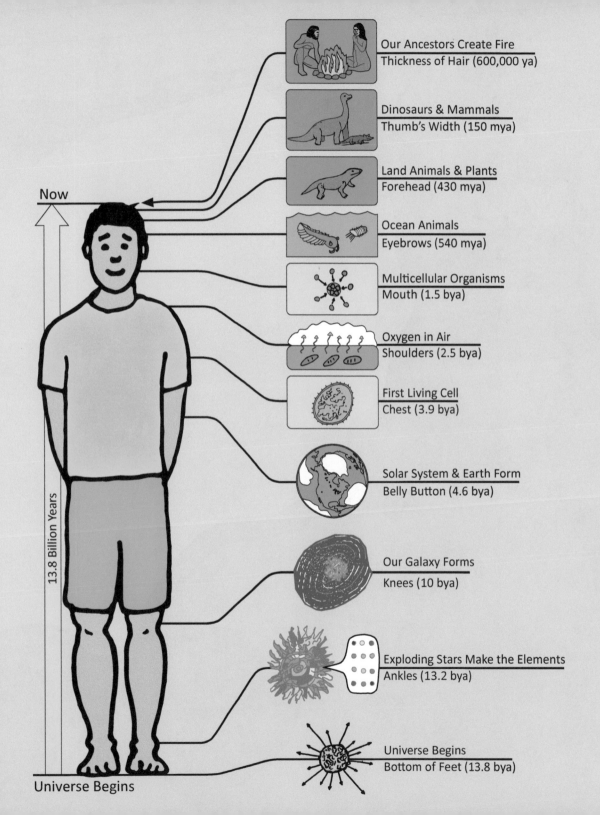

Now

Universe Begins

13.8 Billion Years

Our Ancestors Create Fire
Thickness of Hair (600,000 ya)

Dinosaurs & Mammals
Thumb's Width (150 mya)

Land Animals & Plants
Forehead (430 mya)

Ocean Animals
Eyebrows (540 mya)

Multicellular Organisms
Mouth (1.5 bya)

Oxygen in Air
Shoulders (2.5 bya)

First Living Cell
Chest (3.9 bya)

Solar System & Earth Form
Belly Button (4.6 bya)

Our Galaxy Forms
Knees (10 bya)

Exploding Stars Make the Elements
Ankles (13.2 bya)

Universe Begins
Bottom of Feet (13.8 bya)

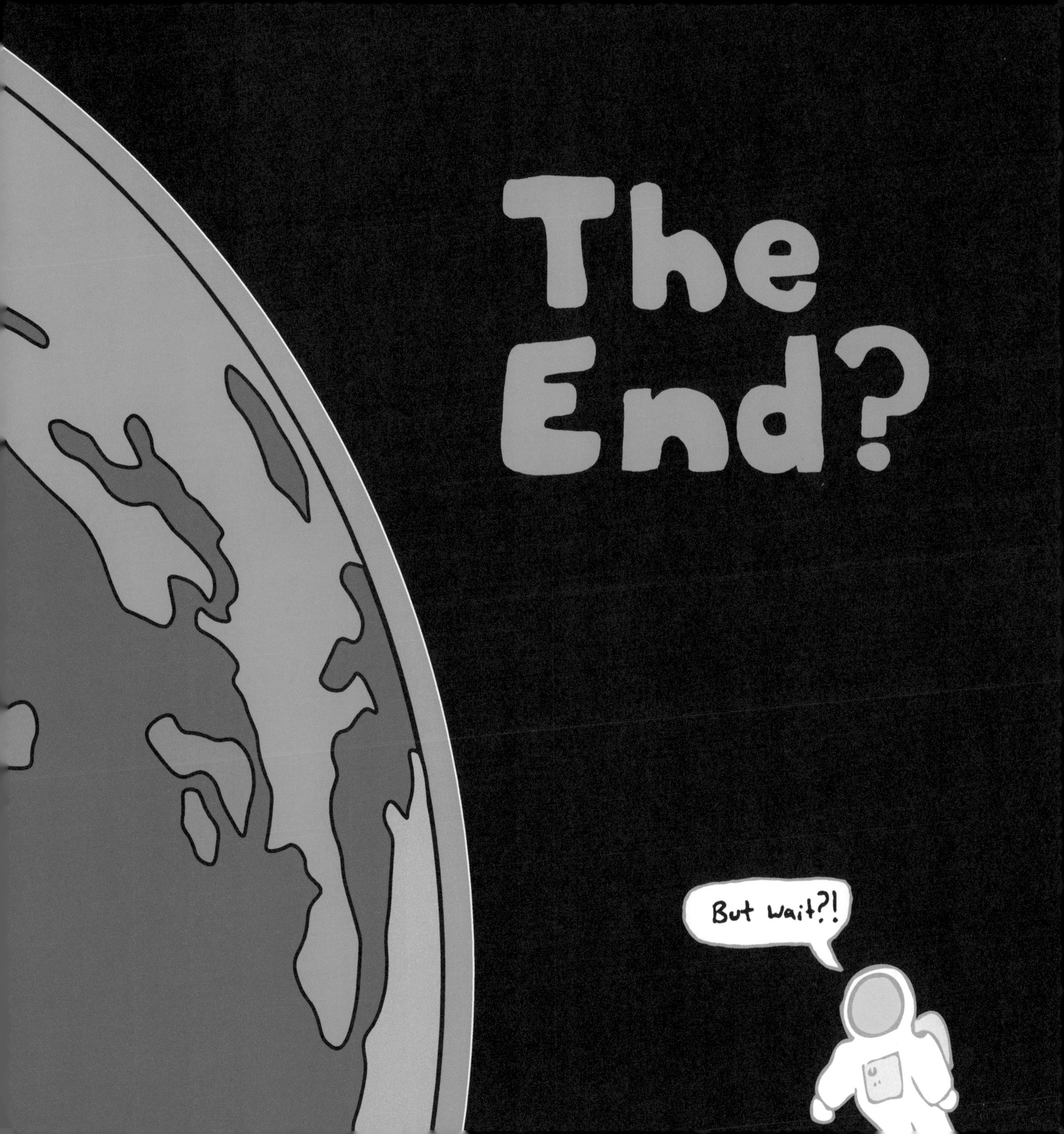
The End?
But wait?!

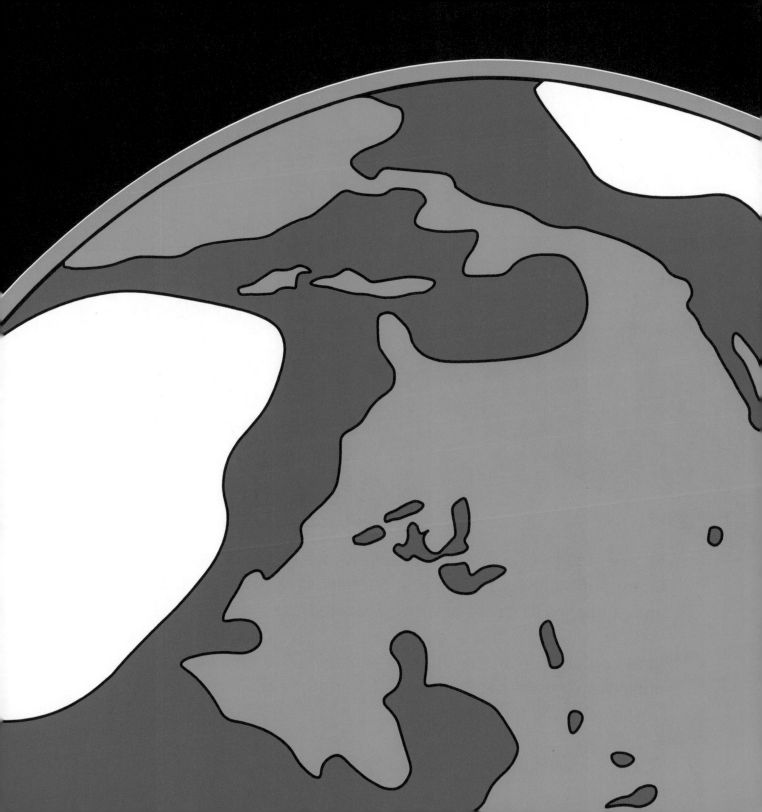

In order to make all our new inventions, we had to use two very important things: our brains and our hands. We used our brains to think, and our hands to create what we imagined.

But in order to do all this thinking and doing, we needed to power ourselves up using the Sun. The Sun's energy gives us oxygen, fresh water, and food.

The Sun powers our planet, which in turn powers every single one of us.

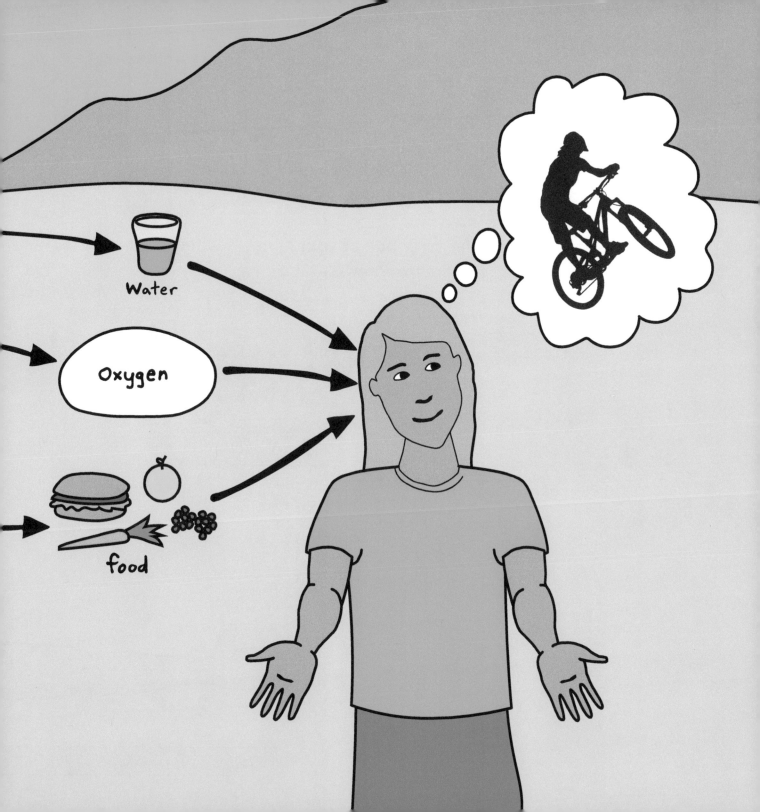

Now stretch out your hands as wide as you can,
so we can see a new timeline.

Imagine that the tip of one of your hands is when
the first farms were invented...

Farms

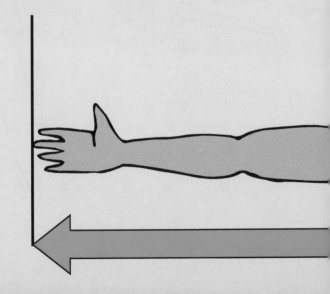

...and the tip of your other hand is now.

This is the timeline of human technology.

Let's look at some of our most important creations and discoveries.

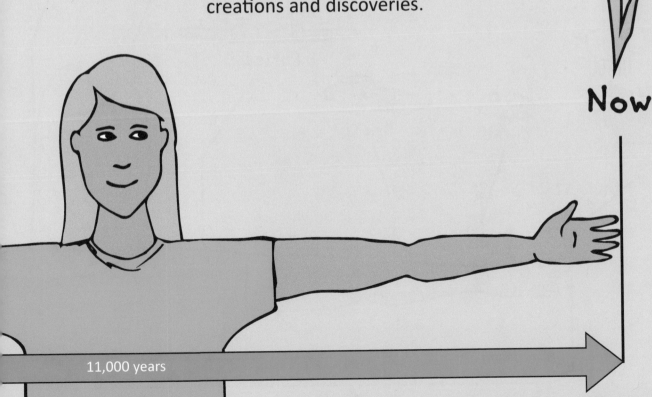

Now

11,000 years

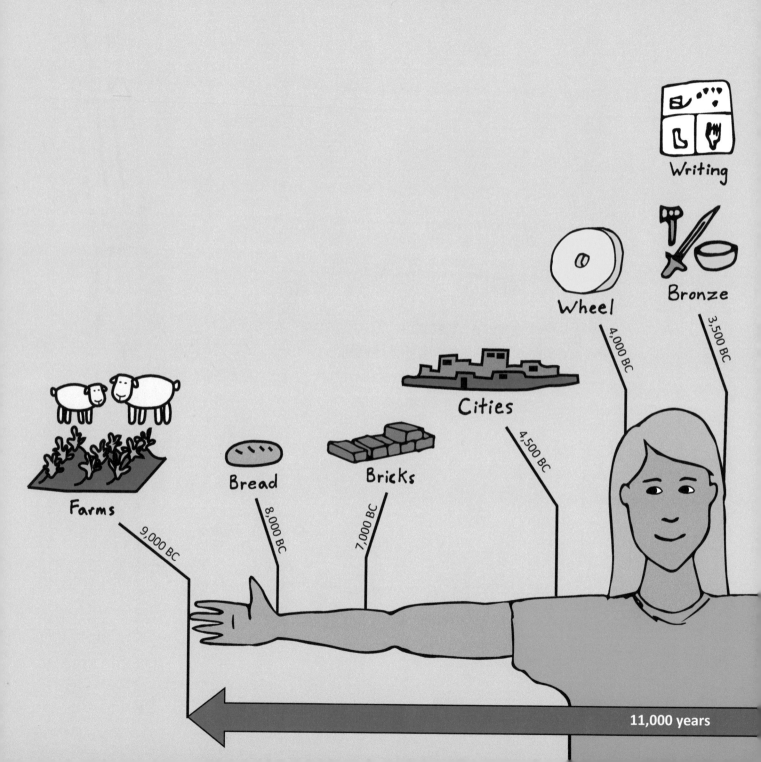

We grew grain in our farms and domesticated animals, like dogs, sheep, and cows. Soon we learned how to grind grain and bake the first bread, by the time we reach your wrist.

We invented bricks, near your elbow, and used them to build buildings. Now that we had lots of food and strong materials, we began building the first cities, which happend at your shoulder.

Cities were powerful places. There, we imagined new ideas and created new inventions.

By the time we reach your two ears, we invented the first wheel, writing and bronze metal. At that time, writing was just simple symbols used to keep track of our more complicated lives. And bronze metal was stronger than any other material we ever had. We could create better tools, swords, and building parts with this amazing metal.

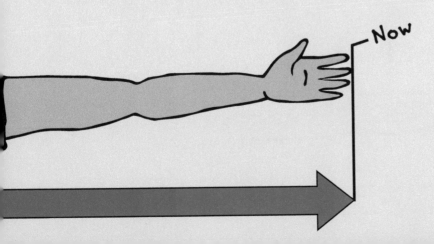
Now

The major religions, still practiced today, were created between your bicep and forearm. These religions, and the religions before them, created a common set of morals in our communities, and helped us live together in even bigger groups.

At your palm, the first printing press was invented, making it easier to create books and share knowledge between people.

Then, Galileo helped show that the Sun was the center of our solar system, at the base of your fingers. Before this, most humans mistakenly believed the Earth was the center of everything. This was the beginning of modern science, which used careful observations and thinking to understand how our world works.

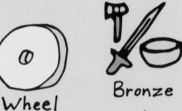

Writing

Wheel

Bronze

4,000 BC

3,500 BC

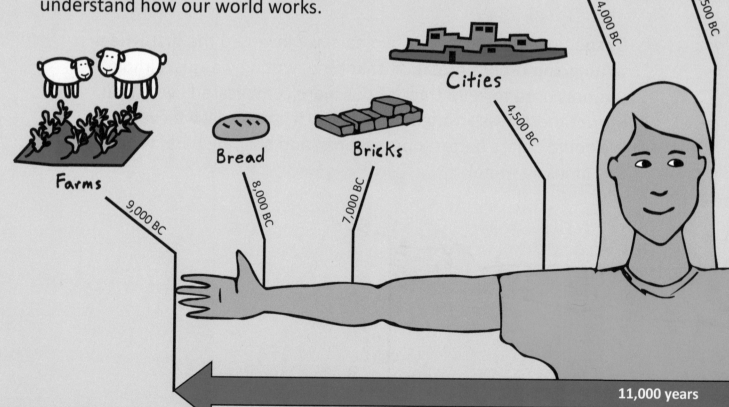

Farms

Bread

Bricks

Cities

4,500 BC

9,000 BC

8,000 BC

7,000 BC

11,000 years

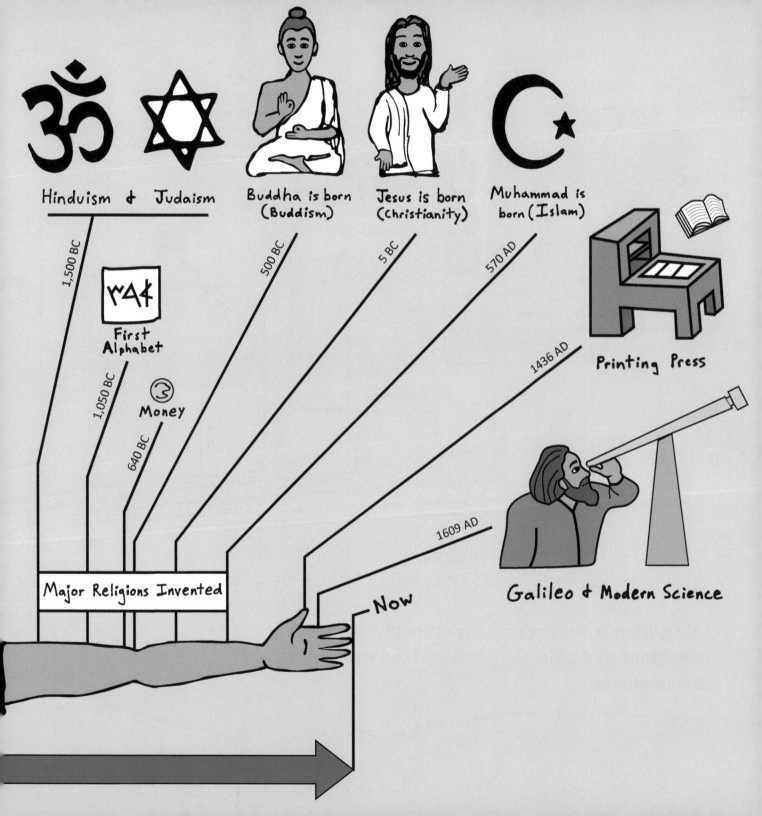

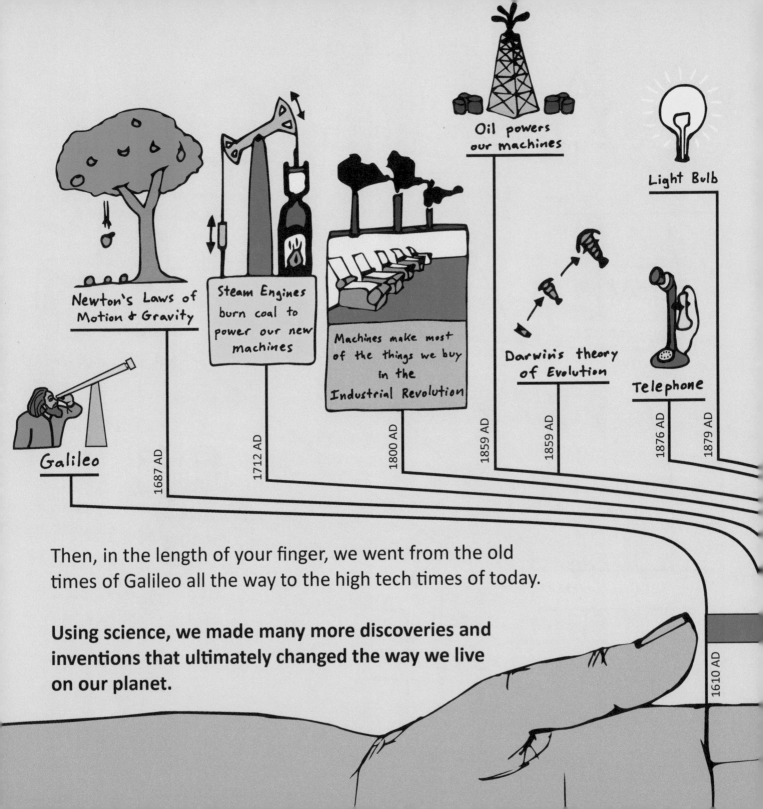

Oil powers
our machines

Light Bulb

Newton's Laws of
Motion & Gravity

Steam Engines
burn coal to
power our new
machines

Machines make most
of the things we buy
in the
Industrial Revolution

Darwin's theory
of Evolution

Telephone

Galileo

1687 AD

1712 AD

1800 AD

1859 AD

1859 AD

1876 AD

1879 AD

Then, in the length of your finger, we went from the old
times of Galileo all the way to the high tech times of today.

**Using science, we made many more discoveries and
inventions that ultimately changed the way we live
on our planet.**

1610 AD

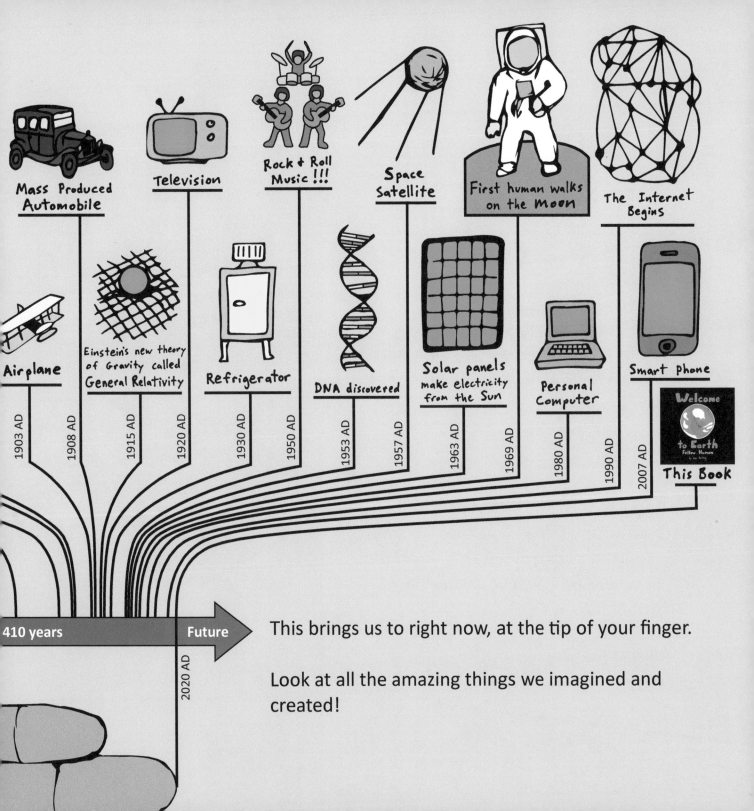

Mass Produced
Automobile

Television

Rock & Roll
Music !!!

Space
Satellite

First human walks
on the Moon

The Internet
Begins

Airplane

Einstein's new theory
of Gravity called
General Relativity

Refrigerator

DNA discovered

Solar panels
make electricity
from the Sun

Personal
Computer

Smart Phone

Welcome
to Earth
Fellow Human
by Leo Bolling

This Book

1903 AD

1908 AD

1915 AD

1920 AD

1930 AD

1950 AD

1953 AD

1957 AD

1963 AD

1969 AD

1980 AD

1990 AD

2007 AD

410 years   Future

2020 AD

This brings us to right now, at the tip of your finger.

Look at all the amazing things we imagined and
created!

Here we are today! It is amazing that everything started out as tiny elements formed long ago. And after billions of years they came together to make our planet, humans, and everything around us.

Now that you see where we came from, it is important to know that as a human there are many things you have no control over. You can't control how big your toes are, or where on Earth you were born.

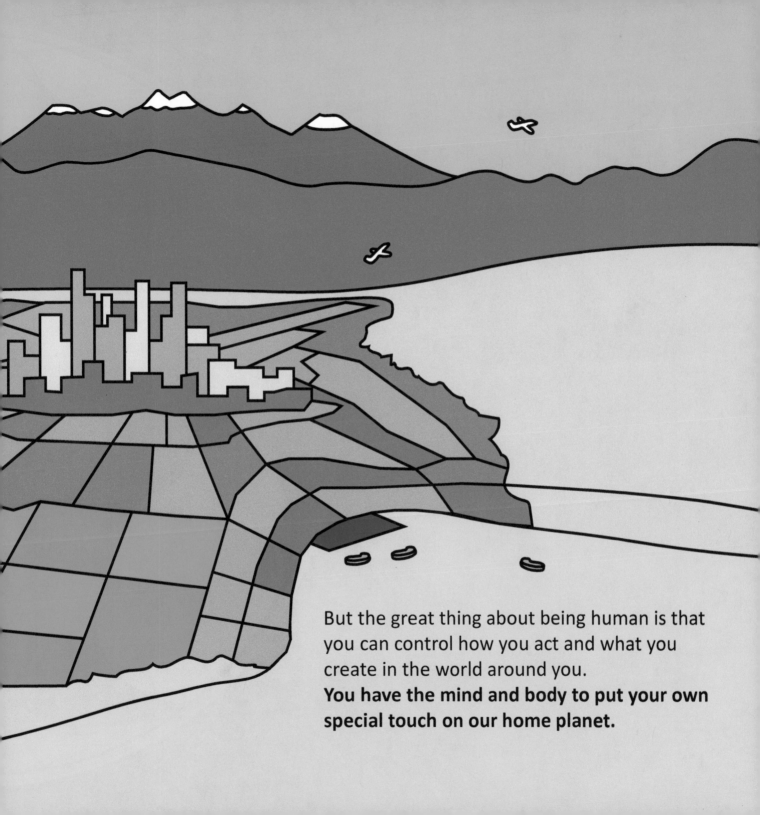

But the great thing about being human is that you can control how you act and what you create in the world around you.
You have the mind and body to put your own special touch on our home planet.

So what will you do with your time on Earth?

What will you create?

Where will you explore?

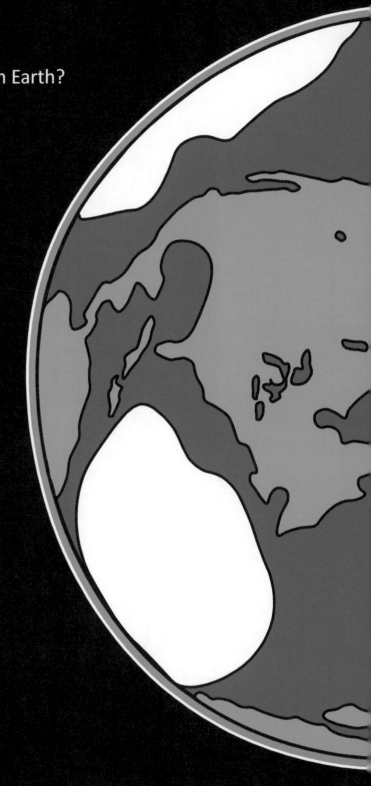

Welcome to Earth!

I hope you make it an awesome place.

Ever since humans evolved on Earth, we have used our minds to try to understand how everything around us works. We learn more and more about the our amazing world each day.

This book is a brief summary of what we've figured out so far about how the Earth and humans came to be.

If you've discovered something that can help make this book better, please let me know. I'd like to keep updating this story as we learn more about the beautiful universe we live in.

Email me at welcometoearthfellowhuman@gmail.com

About the Author

Lee Bolling is a fellow human, husband, father of three, friend, engineer, mathematician, mountain bike shredder, skier, singer-songwriter, singletrack bike trail building visionary and is color blind. He lives in Anchorage, Alaska with his amazing family.

CPSIA information can be obtained
at www.ICGtesting.com
Printed in the USA
BVHW092213121020
590875BV00001B/3